Table Of Contents

Chapter 2: Key Players Behind Dridex 1
Chapter 3: Key Players Behind BitPaymer 1
Chapter 4: The Evolution of Ransomware 1
Chapter 5: Analyzing Dridex..1
Chapter 6: Analyzing BitPaymer...1
Chapter 7: Ransomware as a Service 1
Chapter 8: Incident Response Strategies 1
Chapter 9: Lessons Learned from Dridex and BitPaymer Attacks 1
Chapter 10: Conclusion 1
Chapter 1: Introduction to Evil Corp..1

Chapter 1: Introduction to Evil Corp

Overview of Evil Corp

Evil Corp, a notorious cybercriminal organization, has gained infamy for its role in developing and deploying sophisticated ransomware variants, notably Dridex and BitPaymer. This group operates under a shroud of anonymity, leveraging advanced techniques to perpetrate financial crimes and extort victims worldwide. Originally emerging from Eastern Europe, Evil Corp's operations have expanded globally, targeting a diverse array of sectors, including healthcare, finance, and critical infrastructure. Their ability to continuously adapt and evolve in response to law enforcement efforts and cybersecurity advancements has solidified their position as a formidable threat in the digital landscape.

The group first gained attention with the Dridex banking Trojan, which was primarily designed to steal sensitive financial information. Dridex's modular architecture allowed for the addition of various plugins, enhancing its functionality and enabling it to evade detection. This malware exploited vulnerabilities in Microsoft Office macros to infiltrate systems, making it a particularly potent weapon in the hands of cybercriminals. Over time, Evil Corp transitioned from banking malware to ransomware, culminating in the creation of BitPaymer. This shift marked a significant evolution in their operational strategy, as ransomware offered a more lucrative revenue stream through direct victim payments.

Evil Corp's business model is characterized by the ransomware-as-a-service (RaaS) approach. This model not only democratizes access to ransomware tools but also fosters a broader ecosystem of cybercriminals who may lack the technical expertise to develop their own malware. By renting out their ransomware tools and providing support for other cybercriminals, Evil Corp has effectively scaled its operations, creating a network of affiliates who contribute to their profitability. This collaborative approach has led to an increase in the frequency and severity of ransomware attacks, as a growing number of actors leverage Evil Corp's infrastructure to launch their campaigns.

Incident response to attacks linked to Evil Corp has revealed valuable lessons for cybersecurity professionals. Organizations that have fallen victim to Dridex and BitPaymer ransomware often share common vulnerabilities, such as inadequate security training for employees and a lack of robust backup solutions. Effective incident response requires a comprehensive understanding of the threat landscape, as well as proactive measures to bolster defenses. Implementing multi-factor authentication, regular software updates, and employee education programs can significantly reduce the risk of falling victim to ransomware attacks. Additionally, organizations must develop and test incident response plans to ensure quick recovery in the event of an attack.

In conclusion, Evil Corp represents a significant and evolving threat within the realm of cybersecurity, particularly concerning ransomware attacks. Their history, tactics, and business models provide crucial insights for cybersecurity professionals aiming to defend against these sophisticated adversaries. Understanding the operational framework of Evil Corp, as well as the lessons learned from previous attacks, is essential for developing effective defense strategies and mitigating the impact of ransomware in an increasingly digital world. As the landscape continues to shift, ongoing vigilance and adaptation will be critical in the fight against cybercrime.

Historical Context of Cybercrime

The historical context of cybercrime is essential for understanding the evolution of ransomware and the emergence of notorious groups such as Evil Corp. The roots of cybercrime can be traced back to the late 20th century, when the internet began to gain traction among the general public. Early forms of cybercrime were relatively unsophisticated and largely motivated by curiosity or the challenge of breaching security systems. However, as technology advanced and the internet became a vital part of business operations, cybercriminals began to exploit vulnerabilities for financial gain, laying the groundwork for the complex criminal enterprises we see today.

The turn of the millennium marked a significant shift in the landscape of cybercrime. High-profile incidents, such as the release of the ILOVEYOU virus in 2000, demonstrated the potential for widespread disruption and financial loss. As organizations increasingly relied on digital platforms, the stakes grew higher, prompting criminals to develop more sophisticated techniques. This period saw the rise of various types of malware, including keyloggers and banking Trojans, which would later evolve into the ransomware models represented by Dridex and BitPaymer. The transition from simple hacking to organized cybercrime syndicates marked a pivotal moment in the history of cyber threat actors.

Evil Corp emerged as a prominent player in this evolving landscape, leveraging the growing interconnectedness of networks and the anonymity provided by the dark web. The group capitalized on the rise of Ransomware as a Service (RaaS) models, allowing less technically skilled criminals to deploy sophisticated ransomware attacks with relative ease. The proliferation of such services democratized access to cybercrime tools, enabling a wider range of actors to engage in ransomware attacks. This shift not only increased the frequency of attacks but also escalated the complexity and scale of operations, making groups like Evil Corp key players in the cybercrime ecosystem.

As cybercriminals adopted advanced techniques and targeted organizations with increasing precision, the response from cybersecurity professionals also had to evolve. Organizations became aware of the need for robust incident response strategies, as traditional security measures alone proved insufficient against the sophisticated tactics employed by groups like Evil Corp. The lessons learned from high-profile incidents involving Dridex and BitPaymer highlight the importance of proactive defense measures, continuous monitoring, and the need for a comprehensive understanding of the threat landscape. Cybersecurity teams must remain vigilant and adaptive, recognizing that the tactics used by these groups will continue to evolve.

In conclusion, the historical context of cybercrime is critical for cybersecurity professionals seeking to understand the motivations and methods of groups like Evil Corp. By examining the evolution of ransomware and the role of organized crime in the digital age, professionals can better prepare for future threats. The lessons learned from past incidents underscore the necessity for ongoing education, collaboration, and innovation within the cybersecurity field, as the battle against cybercrime is far from over. Cybersecurity practitioners must stay informed about the changing dynamics of cyber threats to effectively defend against the sophisticated attacks that lie ahead.

Significance of Dridex and BitPaymer

The significance of Dridex and BitPaymer in the landscape of cybersecurity cannot be overstated, particularly as they represent pivotal advancements in ransomware and banking malware. Dridex, originally developed as a banking Trojan, evolved into a formidable ransomware variant that exploits vulnerabilities in both individual and organizational systems. This evolution underscores the adaptability of cybercriminal organizations, particularly Evil Corp, which has leveraged Dridex for financial gain through sophisticated phishing schemes and credential theft. The ability of Dridex to morph into a ransomware delivery mechanism illustrates the interconnected nature of malware and the broader implications for cybersecurity professionals navigating this threat.

BitPaymer, on the other hand, stands as a prime example of ransomware-as-a-service (RaaS) business models that have proliferated in recent years. This model allows even unsophisticated cybercriminals to deploy highly effective ransomware attacks with minimal technical knowledge. By analyzing BitPaymer's operational structure, cybersecurity professionals can gain insights into how these actors package their malware, offer customer support, and facilitate negotiations with victims. The significance of BitPaymer lies not only in its impact on targeted organizations but also in how it exemplifies the commodification of cybercrime, making sophisticated attacks accessible to a wider pool of threat actors.

The operational strategies employed by Evil Corp in deploying Dridex and BitPaymer reveal critical lessons for incident response and cybersecurity defense. Understanding the techniques used for initial infection, lateral movement, and data exfiltration can inform the development of more robust security protocols. Cybersecurity professionals must be aware of the common tactics, techniques, and procedures (TTPs) associated with these threats to enhance their incident response capabilities. The implications extend beyond immediate defense, as organizations must also consider the reputational and financial fallout from such attacks, reinforcing the need for comprehensive risk management strategies.

Moreover, the attacks powered by Dridex and BitPaymer have highlighted the importance of threat intelligence sharing among cybersecurity professionals. As these threats evolve, so too must the strategies to combat them. Collaborative efforts to share indicators of compromise (IoCs), attack patterns, and mitigation strategies can significantly bolster defenses against these sophisticated attacks. The significance of Dridex and BitPaymer extends into the realm of policy-making as well, emphasizing the need for regulatory frameworks that can adapt to the rapid pace of cyber threats, thereby enabling organizations to respond more effectively.

In conclusion, the examination of Dridex and BitPaymer serves as a critical case study for cybersecurity professionals. Their significance lies in the lessons learned about the evolution of malware, the business models underpinning cybercrime, and the necessary responses to mitigate their impact. As the threat landscape continues to evolve, an understanding of these ransomware variants will be essential for developing effective strategies to protect against future attacks. Cybersecurity professionals must remain vigilant, informed, and adaptable in the face of these ongoing challenges.

Chapter 2: Key Players Behind Dridex

Origins of Dridex

The origins of Dridex can be traced back to the broader context of cybercrime that emerged in the late 2000s. Initially, Dridex was identified as a banking Trojan, primarily targeting financial institutions and their customers. Its creators harnessed the growing sophistication of malware development, leveraging existing vulnerabilities in both software and human behavior. This period saw an increase in online banking activity, which provided fertile ground for cybercriminals. As users became more reliant on digital banking, the need for effective tools to exploit this trend became evident, leading to the birth of Dridex.

Dridex's architecture is rooted in modular design, allowing it to evolve rapidly in response to security measures. The malware was first seen in 2014, but its development was informed by prior threats such as Zeus and SpyEye. By borrowing techniques from these earlier Trojans, Dridex was able to introduce innovative features that enhanced its stealth and effectiveness. The malware utilized a peer-to-peer network for command and control (C2) operations, which made it more resilient against takedown efforts by law enforcement and cybersecurity professionals. This adaptability has been a key factor in its proliferation and ongoing relevance in the cybercriminal landscape.

The operational model of Dridex has undergone significant evolution, particularly in its transition to a ransomware model through the association with BitPaymer. Initially, Dridex focused on credential theft, but as the cyber threat environment shifted, the operators began to integrate ransomware functionalities. This shift represented a strategic pivot that allowed the group behind Dridex to monetize their efforts more effectively. By demanding ransoms in cryptocurrencies, they capitalized on the anonymity provided by digital currencies, thus creating a sustainable revenue stream while minimizing the risks associated with traditional financial transactions.

The rise of Dridex also reflects the emergence of Ransomware as a Service (RaaS) models. This business model democratized access to sophisticated malware, enabling less technically skilled cybercriminals to engage in ransomware attacks. The Dridex operators effectively commodified their malware, offering it to affiliates who could launch their own attacks in exchange for a cut of the profits. This approach not only expanded the reach of Dridex but also contributed to a surge in ransomware incidents globally, as more attackers adopted the framework laid out by Evil Corp and similar organizations.

Understanding the origins and evolution of Dridex is crucial for cybersecurity professionals tasked with incident response and threat mitigation. The lessons learned from previous Dridex and BitPaymer attacks highlight the importance of proactive measures, including robust user education on phishing tactics, network segmentation, and timely software updates. As the threat landscape continues to evolve, staying informed about the origins and operational strategies of malware like Dridex will be essential in developing effective defenses against future cyber threats.

Major Figures in Dridex Development

The development of Dridex, a notorious banking Trojan, is attributed to a handful of key figures whose expertise and strategic vision have shaped its evolution. Among these figures is an individual known by the online alias "Bledsoe." His role as a lead developer has been pivotal in enhancing Dridex's capabilities, allowing it to adapt to various security measures. Bledsoe's technical acumen in malware development has enabled Dridex to maintain its relevance in the ever-evolving landscape of cyber threats. His contributions include the implementation of sophisticated evasion techniques, making detection by traditional security systems increasingly challenging.

Another significant figure in the Dridex ecosystem is "Dmitry," a well-known figure in the underground cybercrime community. Dmitry has been instrumental in establishing the operational framework for Dridex's distribution networks. Under his guidance, Dridex has leveraged social engineering tactics and phishing campaigns to infiltrate targeted organizations. Dmitry's insights into human behavior have allowed the group to refine their attack vectors, maximizing the Trojan's effectiveness. His understanding of the cybersecurity landscape has also driven continuous updates to Dridex, ensuring that it remains a formidable threat.

The role of "Vlad," a former security researcher turned cybercriminal, cannot be overlooked in the context of Dridex development. Vlad's expertise in cybersecurity was initially employed to bolster defenses, but his shift to the dark side has provided him with unique insights into both offensive and defensive strategies. His involvement in the Dridex project has been marked by the integration of advanced techniques such as modular architecture and dynamic payload delivery, which enhance the Trojan's adaptability and reduce its footprint on infected systems. Vlad's dual perspective fosters a cycle of innovation within the group that keeps them ahead of cybersecurity professionals.

The collaborative nature of these major figures has led to the establishment of a cohesive team within the Dridex development community. Alongside Bledsoe, Dmitry, and Vlad, other contributors include skilled coders and experienced marketers who are responsible for promoting the malware and its infrastructure. This synergy has resulted in a robust Ransomware-as-a-Service (RaaS) model, where affiliate partnerships enable the rapid dissemination of Dridex. The team's combined expertise not only drives the technical enhancements of the Trojan but also facilitates its distribution, allowing for a wider reach and greater financial gain.

As cybersecurity professionals study the evolution of Dridex and its associated figures, important lessons emerge regarding incident response and threat mitigation. Understanding the motivations and methodologies of these key players can inform security strategies, helping organizations to anticipate potential threats and develop proactive measures. The insights gained from analyzing the development of Dridex highlight the importance of continual adaptation in cybersecurity practices, emphasizing the need for ongoing education and collaboration within the industry to counteract the sophisticated tactics employed by cybercriminals.

Roles and Responsibilities within Evil Corp

The operational structure of Evil Corp is a complex web of roles and responsibilities that facilitate the execution of its nefarious activities. At the helm of this organization is the leadership team, which consists of high-ranking cybercriminals who strategize the overall direction and objectives of the group's operations. These individuals are not only responsible for planning large-scale attacks but also for securing partnerships with other cybercriminal entities. Their experience in cybercrime allows them to effectively manage the various components of the organization, ensuring that each arm of the operation functions cohesively.

Beneath the leadership team, the technical specialists play a crucial role in the development and deployment of the Dridex and BitPaymer malware. These individuals possess advanced skills in programming and network security, enabling them to create sophisticated ransomware that can evade detection by traditional security measures. Their responsibilities include writing the malware code, testing its effectiveness, and continuously updating the software to exploit new vulnerabilities. This technical expertise is vital for maintaining the operational effectiveness of Evil Corp's ransomware, as it directly impacts the success of their attacks.

Another critical aspect of Evil Corp's structure is the operational team, which is tasked with executing attacks and managing the logistics involved. This includes reconnaissance on potential targets, deploying the ransomware, and ensuring that the attack is carried out smoothly. The operational team must also communicate effectively with the leadership to align their execution with the group's strategic goals. Their role is often high-pressure, as they must adapt to changing circumstances and respond to any unforeseen obstacles during an attack, all while remaining anonymous and avoiding capture.

The support staff within Evil Corp also plays a significant role in maintaining the organization's infrastructure. This includes individuals responsible for managing the servers and communication channels used for command and control. They ensure that the ransomware can be deployed without interruptions and that payment channels remain secure. Additionally, they may handle customer support for victims, guiding them through the ransom payment process. This aspect of the organization highlights the business model behind Evil Corp, where customer service is tailored to enhance the likelihood of successful ransom payments.

Lastly, the intelligence and research division focuses on gathering information about potential targets, industry trends, and developments in cybersecurity defenses. This team analyzes past attacks to refine strategies and improve the effectiveness of future operations. Their insights help shape the tactical decisions made by the leadership and operational teams, ensuring that Evil Corp remains a step ahead of law enforcement and cybersecurity professionals. Understanding the interplay between these roles and responsibilities provides valuable insights into the inner workings of Evil Corp and the evolution of ransomware as a service.

Chapter 3: Key Players Behind BitPaymer

Origins of BitPaymer

BitPaymer emerged as a significant player in the ransomware landscape, tracing its origins back to the activities of a group known as Evil Corp. This criminal organization gained notoriety through its development and distribution of various malware strains, with Dridex being one of the most prominent examples. Dridex, primarily a banking Trojan, laid the groundwork for BitPaymer by establishing a network of compromised machines that could be leveraged for larger-scale attacks. The evolution from Dridex to BitPaymer reflects a strategic pivot in the group's operations, shifting from direct financial theft to a more sophisticated ransomware model.

The first recorded instances of BitPaymer surfaced around 2017, marking a period when ransomware attacks began to escalate in frequency and severity. What set BitPaymer apart was its targeted approach, often focusing on high-profile organizations that could afford to pay significant ransoms. This targeted strategy was rooted in the operational tactics used in previous attacks, where Evil Corp had gathered intelligence on potential victims through the use of Dridex. The ransomware would encrypt files on compromised systems, demanding payment in Bitcoin, which added a layer of anonymity for the attackers.

BitPaymer operated on a Ransomware as a Service (RaaS) model, allowing other cybercriminals to deploy the ransomware against their own targets in exchange for a share of the ransom payments. This business model not only broadened the reach of BitPaymer but also contributed to its proliferation across various industries. The RaaS structure enabled Evil Corp to scale its operations, attracting a network of affiliates who were eager to exploit the ransomware's capabilities. This collaborative approach significantly increased the volume of attacks and the potential for profit, positioning BitPaymer as a formidable threat in the cybersecurity landscape.

The sophistication of BitPaymer's design and distribution methods played a crucial role in its success. The malware was often delivered via phishing emails, leveraging social engineering tactics to trick users into executing the malicious payload. Once inside a network, BitPaymer would utilize lateral movement techniques to infect additional systems, maximizing its impact before encryption occurred. The encryption process itself was robust, utilizing strong algorithms that made recovery without paying the ransom nearly impossible, further incentivizing victims to comply with the demands set by Evil Corp.

The rise of BitPaymer serves as a case study in the evolution of ransomware tactics and the complexities of incident response in the face of such threats. Cybersecurity professionals must analyze the operational strategies employed by Evil Corp to understand how similar groups might evolve in the future. Lessons learned from incidents involving BitPaymer highlight the importance of proactive measures, including employee training, robust backup solutions, and effective incident response plans. As ransomware continues to adapt, staying informed about its origins and developments is crucial for building resilient defenses against this pervasive threat.

Major Figures in BitPaymer Development

In the landscape of ransomware development, BitPaymer stands out as a significant player, primarily due to the contributions of several key figures within its development team. These individuals were not only skilled programmers but also adept in understanding the evolving dynamics of cybersecurity and cybercrime. Their collective expertise allowed them to create a ransomware variant that was both sophisticated and effective. Among these figures, the lead developer, known by the pseudonym "Aldrich," played a pivotal role in the initial coding and architecture of BitPaymer, ensuring that it could evade detection by leading antivirus solutions while still being user-friendly for cybercriminal affiliates.

Another major figure in the development of BitPaymer is "Tarn," who specialized in the monetization strategies that accompanied the ransomware's deployment. Tarn's background in financial technology allowed him to integrate sophisticated payment systems within the ransomware, making it easier for victims to pay ransoms using cryptocurrencies. This emphasis on efficient payment processing not only increased the likelihood of payments but also allowed for the seamless laundering of funds, which is crucial for the sustainability of ransomware operations. Tarn's insights into market trends helped shape BitPaymer's pricing strategies, appealing to a broad range of potential victims.

The role of "Viktor," a cybersecurity expert turned cybercriminal, cannot be overlooked in the context of BitPaymer's development. Viktor's understanding of defensive measures employed by organizations enabled the team to craft features that specifically targeted vulnerabilities in enterprise environments. His contributions included the development of lateral movement tactics and the deployment of advanced encryption methods that rendered data recovery nearly impossible without the decryption key. This strategic focus on penetrating corporate defenses significantly enhanced the effectiveness of BitPaymer, making it a preferred choice among affiliates.

Additionally, the involvement of a collective known as the "Evil Corp Syndicate" provided a support structure that facilitated the growth and reach of BitPaymer. This group comprised various hackers and affiliates who specialized in different aspects of ransomware deployment, from initial access acquisition to customer support for victims. Their collaborative approach allowed for rapid iterations and adaptations of the ransomware, ensuring that it remained competitive in an ever-evolving landscape of cybersecurity threats. This synergy among various specialists contributed to BitPaymer's notoriety and effectiveness.

Finally, the interplay between these major figures and their respective roles illustrates the complex ecosystem behind BitPaymer's development. Each individual brought unique skills and perspectives, creating a multifaceted organization capable of both innovation and operational efficiency. Understanding the contributions of these key players is essential for cybersecurity professionals seeking to comprehend the mechanisms behind ransomware as a service and the broader implications for incident response strategies. By analyzing the collaborative efforts that led to the creation of BitPaymer, professionals can better prepare for the challenges posed by ransomware threats in the future.

Roles and Responsibilities within Evil Corp

Understanding the roles and responsibilities within Evil Corp is crucial for cybersecurity professionals aiming to dissect the operational framework of one of the most notorious cybercriminal organizations. Each member of this group plays a pivotal role in the development, deployment, and maintenance of their ransomware products, such as Dridex and BitPaymer. The organization operates with a hierarchical structure, where leadership oversees strategic planning, while various teams focus on the technical, financial, and operational aspects of their criminal enterprise.

At the top of the hierarchy are the masterminds or architects of Evil Corp, who are responsible for designing the ransomware and creating the overarching strategy for its distribution. These individuals possess advanced technical skills and a deep understanding of cybersecurity vulnerabilities, which they exploit to enhance their malware's effectiveness. Their vision dictates the development of new features in ransomware, adapting to countermeasures implemented by cybersecurity professionals and law enforcement agencies.

Supporting the architects are the developers, who write and maintain the actual code of the ransomware. This group is tasked with continuously evolving the malware to evade detection and improve its capabilities. They work on updates and patches, ensuring that the ransomware remains functional despite attempts at mitigation by security software. Their expertise in programming languages and familiarity with various operating systems allow them to create sophisticated ransomware variants that can infiltrate a wide array of targets.

Another crucial role within Evil Corp is that of the distributors. These individuals specialize in the marketing and dissemination of the ransomware. They leverage various tactics, including phishing campaigns and exploit kits, to deliver the malware to potential victims. Distributors often work in tandem with affiliate programs, allowing them to extend the reach of their ransomware by enabling other cybercriminals to use Evil Corp's products in exchange for a share of the ransom payments. This model of Ransomware as a

Service underscores the organization's business-oriented approach to cybercrime.

Finally, the financial operatives play a significant role in managing the profits generated from ransomware attacks. These individuals are responsible for laundering the ransom payments, often using complex networks of cryptocurrency transactions to obscure the origins of the funds. They understand the intricacies of financial systems and leverage anonymizing services to ensure that the profits are discreetly reinvested or accessed. The seamless collaboration among these roles within Evil Corp highlights the sophisticated and organized nature of their operations, providing vital insights for cybersecurity professionals working to combat such threats.

Chapter 4: The Evolution of Ransomware

Early Forms of Ransomware

The emergence of ransomware dates back to the late 1980s, with early iterations laying the groundwork for the sophisticated attacks seen today. The first known ransomware, known as the "AIDS Trojan" or "PC Cyborg," was released in 1989. Distributed via floppy disks, it encrypted files on infected systems and demanded a payment to restore access. This early form of ransomware set a precedent for future attacks, showcasing how cybercriminals could leverage encryption as a mechanism for monetization. Its primitive nature, however, meant that it was relatively easy to circumvent, as victims could simply delete the infected files and restore from backups.

As the internet became more accessible throughout the 1990s, ransomware began to evolve. The rise of email as a primary communication tool for both individuals and businesses provided a new vector for ransomware distribution. Variants like "Gpcoder" began to appear, utilizing more sophisticated encryption techniques and targeting specific file types to maximize impact. This transition marked a shift in ransomware's operational models, as attackers started to recognize the potential for greater financial gain by targeting larger organizations with critical data. The introduction of social engineering tactics, particularly through phishing emails, became a hallmark of these early ransomware attacks.

The early 2000s saw a surge in ransomware variants, including "Gpcode" and "Cryzip." These versions introduced more complex encryption algorithms, making it increasingly difficult for victims to recover their data without paying the ransom. Cybercriminals began to refine their tactics, using increasingly aggressive methods to coerce victims into compliance. The shift towards targeting businesses rather than individuals indicated a strategic evolution in the ransomware landscape, as attackers recognized that organizations were more likely to pay substantial ransoms to avoid operational disruptions. This change in focus also prompted discussions among cybersecurity professionals regarding the importance of robust incident response strategies.

By the mid-2000s, the introduction of the "Ransomware-as-a-Service" (RaaS) model marked a significant turning point in the ransomware ecosystem. This model enabled even novice cybercriminals to launch ransomware attacks, democratizing access to sophisticated tools and techniques. RaaS platforms provided attackers with user-friendly interfaces and support, allowing them to customize their attacks without extensive technical knowledge. This proliferation of ransomware tools contributed to a dramatic increase in the frequency and scale of attacks, making it imperative for cybersecurity professionals to develop comprehensive strategies for detection, prevention, and response.

The evolution of early ransomware forms laid the foundation for the more complex and lucrative operations associated with Dridex and BitPaymer. Understanding these historical contexts helps cybersecurity professionals appreciate the ongoing challenges in combating ransomware today. As the tactics and techniques of cybercriminals continue to evolve, so must the strategies employed by defenders. Lessons learned from past incidents emphasize the need for continuous improvement in incident response protocols and the importance of fostering a culture of cybersecurity awareness within organizations to mitigate the risks posed by ransomware.

Transition to Dridex and BitPaymer

The transition to Dridex and BitPaymer marks a significant evolution in the landscape of ransomware, representing a shift in tactics, technology, and operational strategy employed by cybercriminals. Initially, Dridex emerged as a banking Trojan, primarily targeting financial institutions and their customers. This malware exploited vulnerabilities to steal credentials and facilitate fraudulent transactions. However, the developers recognized the potential of leveraging such infections to deploy ransomware, leading to the evolution of Dridex into a more versatile tool. By incorporating ransomware capabilities, Dridex transitioned from a mere data thief to a formidable threat in the growing ransomware-as-a-service ecosystem.

BitPaymer, on the other hand, was developed as a dedicated ransomware strain, designed to encrypt files and demand payment in cryptocurrency for decryption keys. Its emergence illustrated a clear understanding of market demands and the evolving tactics of cybercriminals. BitPaymer's operational model showcased an effective combination of stealth and aggression, often utilizing initial access gained from other malware like Dridex to execute its ransomware payload. This synergy between the two threats not only amplified their reach but also underscored a strategic partnership in the cybercriminal underground, where tools and tactics are shared to maximize profitability.

The business model of Evil Corp, the group behind Dridex and BitPaymer, reflects the maturation of ransomware operations. By adopting a ransomware-as-a-service model, they enabled even less technically skilled criminals to launch sophisticated attacks. This democratization of ransomware has led to an explosion in attacks, as affiliates can leverage Dridex and BitPaymer's capabilities without needing extensive expertise. The financial incentives are significant; successful attacks can yield substantial ransoms, while the initial infrastructure and development costs are relatively low, making the business model highly attractive to a wide array of cybercriminals.

From an incident response perspective, the lessons learned from Dridex and BitPaymer attacks are critical for cybersecurity professionals. The dual nature of these threats emphasizes the need for organizations to adopt a holistic approach to cybersecurity that encompasses both prevention and response. Regular updates to security protocols, employee training on phishing awareness, and robust backup solutions are essential elements in defending against such evolving threats. Additionally, understanding the operational tactics of these ransomware variants helps in preemptively identifying potential vulnerabilities within an organization, allowing for a more proactive stance against cyber threats.

In conclusion, the transition to Dridex and BitPaymer exemplifies the dynamic nature of ransomware and the continual adaptation of cybercriminals to exploit weaknesses in security infrastructures. For cybersecurity professionals, this evolution serves as a reminder of the ongoing arms race between attackers and defenders. By staying informed about the latest developments in ransomware tactics and maintaining a strong incident response framework, organizations can better protect themselves from the sophisticated threats posed by Evil Corp and similar entities in the evolving cyber threat landscape.

Technological Advancements and Tactics

Technological advancements have played a crucial role in the evolution of ransomware, particularly in the case of Dridex and BitPaymer, two of the most notorious strains attributed to Evil Corp. These advancements have not only facilitated the development of sophisticated malware but have also enabled attackers to leverage new tactics that enhance their effectiveness. The integration of machine learning and artificial intelligence into malware design allows for adaptive strategies, enabling cybercriminals to bypass traditional security measures and exploit vulnerabilities in real-time.

Dridex, initially designed as a banking Trojan, illustrates the shift in tactics employed by cybercriminals. Its evolution into a ransomware variant exemplifies how attackers have adapted to the changing landscape of cybersecurity. By utilizing advanced obfuscation techniques and leveraging peer-to-peer architecture, Dridex makes detection and mitigation increasingly challenging for security professionals. The ability of Dridex to deploy additional payloads and execute lateral movement within networks underscores the importance of understanding these technological innovations and their implications for incident response.

BitPaymer, on the other hand, has adopted a Ransomware-as-a-Service (RaaS) model, which has transformed the operational dynamics of ransomware distribution. This model allows various affiliates to access the ransomware toolkit, thereby expanding its reach and increasing the frequency of attacks. The incorporation of payment systems that facilitate anonymous transactions adds another layer of complexity, as it enables attackers to monetize their efforts while minimizing the risk of detection. Cybersecurity professionals must recognize this shift towards a service-oriented approach and adjust their strategies accordingly to counter these threats.

The tactics employed by Evil Corp are not limited to technical innovations; they also encompass social engineering techniques that exploit human vulnerabilities. Phishing campaigns, which often serve as the initial vector for both Dridex and BitPaymer infections, have become more sophisticated and targeted. By employing tailored messages that resonate with specific individuals or organizations, attackers significantly increase the likelihood of successful breaches. Cybersecurity professionals must prioritize user education and awareness as a crucial component of their defense strategies to mitigate the risks associated with these social engineering tactics.

In conclusion, the interplay between technological advancements and evolving tactics highlights the dynamic nature of the ransomware landscape. Cybersecurity professionals must remain vigilant and proactive in adapting their defenses to counteract the innovative methods employed by Evil Corp and its affiliates. Continuous monitoring of emerging threats, investment in advanced security technologies, and fostering a culture of security awareness within organizations are essential steps in effectively combating the persistent threat of ransomware, as exemplified by Dridex and BitPaymer.

Chapter 5: Analyzing Dridex

Technical Architecture of Dridex

The technical architecture of Dridex is a complex framework that underscores its effectiveness as a banking trojan and ransomware delivery system. At its core, Dridex is designed to infiltrate systems, exfiltrate sensitive information, and facilitate additional payloads, such as ransomware like BitPaymer. The architecture is modular, allowing for various components to interact seamlessly, enhancing its adaptability and resilience against detection. This flexibility is crucial for evading cybersecurity measures and ensuring the trojan's persistence within compromised networks.

Dridex employs a multi-layered approach to communication, utilizing a combination of command and control (C2) servers, peer-to-peer protocols, and web-based APIs. The trojan typically communicates with its C2 servers via encrypted channels, which helps obfuscate its traffic and evade network monitoring solutions. In addition to standard HTTP/S communication, Dridex can utilize other protocols, such as DNS tunneling, to maintain a stealthy presence. The use of these various communication methods allows Dridex to receive commands, update its functionalities, and transmit stolen data without raising alarms.

The infection process of Dridex is primarily initiated through phishing campaigns, often leveraging malicious email attachments or links. Once a user inadvertently executes the malicious payload, Dridex deploys a series of obfuscation techniques to evade detection by antivirus and endpoint protection solutions. The initial payload is designed to establish a foothold on the victim's system, often by disabling security features and creating persistence mechanisms that ensure the malware remains active even after system reboots. This stage is critical for maintaining control over the infected environment.

Once established, Dridex can download additional modules that extend its capabilities, including keyloggers, form grabbers, and ransomware payloads like BitPaymer. These modules work in concert to gather sensitive information, such as login credentials and financial data, which can be exploited for financial gain or sold on underground markets. The ransomware component is particularly concerning, as it can encrypt files across the network, demanding a ransom for decryption keys. This dual functionality not only amplifies the threat posed by Dridex but also reflects the evolving nature of ransomware as a service.

Understanding the technical architecture of Dridex is paramount for cybersecurity professionals tasked with defending against such threats. It highlights the importance of implementing layered security strategies that include user education, robust email filtering, and endpoint protection technologies. Additionally, incident response teams must be equipped to identify the signs of Dridex infections early to mitigate the damage and prevent further propagation. By dissecting the architecture of Dridex, cybersecurity experts can better prepare for the evolving landscape of ransomware threats and develop more effective countermeasures.

Attack Vectors and Delivery Methods

Understanding the attack vectors and delivery methods employed by Evil Corp is crucial for cybersecurity professionals tasked with defending against sophisticated threats like Dridex and BitPaymer ransomware. The primary vector for these attacks often involves social engineering techniques, such as phishing emails. These emails are meticulously crafted to appear legitimate, tricking recipients into opening malicious attachments or clicking on links leading to compromised websites. Once a victim interacts with the payload, the malware can be executed, leading to a breach that compromises sensitive data and systems.

Another significant delivery method utilized by Evil Corp is the exploitation of vulnerabilities in software and operating systems. Cybercriminals often leverage known vulnerabilities that have not been patched by organizations, taking advantage of outdated systems to deploy ransomware silently. This approach is particularly effective in environments where security updates are not regularly applied, allowing for a stealthy entry point into corporate networks. By exploiting these weaknesses, attackers can gain the necessary foothold to escalate privileges and deploy ransomware across various networked devices.

In addition to phishing and exploit-based attacks, Evil Corp has also adopted a strategy focused on the use of malicious advertisements, commonly referred to as malvertising. This method involves embedding ransomware payloads within seemingly harmless advertisements on legitimate websites. When a user clicks on or even views these ads, malicious code is executed, leading to the installation of ransomware without any direct interaction with the user. This delivery method underscores the importance of comprehensive web filtering and the use of ad blockers as part of a multi-layered security strategy.

Moreover, leveraging remote desktop protocol (RDP) vulnerabilities has become a common tactic for Evil Corp affiliates. By brute-forcing weak passwords or exploiting misconfigurations, attackers can gain access to systems remotely. Once inside, they can deploy ransomware across the network, often leading to widespread disruption and significant financial losses. This highlights the critical need for organizations to implement strong password policies, enable two-factor authentication, and monitor RDP access to mitigate such risks effectively.

Finally, the rise of Ransomware as a Service (RaaS) has expanded the delivery methods available to cybercriminals. This model allows even less technically skilled criminals to launch sophisticated attacks by purchasing access to ransomware kits and associated services. As a result, the threat landscape has become more diverse, with various affiliates using different attack vectors and delivery methods tailored to their specific targets. Cybersecurity professionals must remain vigilant and adaptive, continuously updating their defenses and response strategies to counter these evolving tactics employed by Evil Corp and similar threat actors.

Impact of Dridex on Organizations

The impact of Dridex on organizations has been profound, affecting not only the immediate financial stability of targeted entities but also their long-term operational integrity. Dridex, primarily a banking Trojan, has evolved into a multifaceted threat that enables cybercriminals to execute a range of malicious activities, including data theft and ransomware deployment. Its ability to bypass traditional security measures through sophisticated techniques, such as social engineering and evasion tactics, has made it a formidable adversary for organizations of all sizes. As organizations adapt to the evolving threat landscape, understanding the implications of Dridex is crucial for enhancing their cybersecurity posture.

One of the most significant impacts of Dridex is the financial burden it places on organizations. The direct costs associated with a Dridex infection can be staggering, including remediation expenses, potential ransom payments, and lost revenue due to operational downtime. Furthermore, the indirect costs, such as reputational damage and diminished customer trust, can have lasting effects on a company's market position. Organizations often find themselves grappling with the aftermath of an attack, which may involve regulatory fines and increased scrutiny from stakeholders, thereby intensifying the long-term financial repercussions.

In addition to financial implications, the operational impact of Dridex can disrupt business continuity. Once embedded within an organization's infrastructure, Dridex can facilitate lateral movement across networks, compromising critical systems and sensitive data. This disruption can hinder daily operations and necessitate extensive incident response efforts. Organizations must invest in robust incident response plans that not only address immediate threats but also incorporate lessons learned from past experiences with Dridex and similar malware. Failure to prepare adequately can result in prolonged recovery times and increased vulnerability to future attacks.

The psychological impact on employees and leadership cannot be overlooked. The fear of a potential cyber breach can create a culture of anxiety and mistrust within an organization. Employees may become hesitant to engage with digital tools or share information, leading to decreased productivity and morale. Additionally, leadership teams face the challenge of maintaining stakeholder confidence while navigating the complexities of a cyber incident. This can strain internal resources and divert attention from strategic business initiatives, further compounding the negative effects of a Dridex infection.

Finally, the evolving nature of Dridex underscores the importance of continuous vigilance and adaptation in cybersecurity practices. Organizations must stay informed about the latest tactics employed by cybercriminals and invest in advanced security solutions that can detect and mitigate threats in real time. Collaborative efforts among cybersecurity professionals, information sharing, and threat intelligence are essential in combating the pervasive influence of Dridex. By fostering a proactive cybersecurity culture and leveraging insights from past incidents, organizations can better protect themselves against the multifaceted threats posed by Dridex and similar ransomware-as-a-service models.

Chapter 6: Analyzing BitPaymer

Technical Architecture of BitPaymer

The technical architecture of BitPaymer ransomware represents a sophisticated blend of various components designed to optimize its functionality and enhance its evasion tactics against detection. At its core, BitPaymer is built upon a modular framework that allows for dynamic adaptability in its operation. This modularity enables the attackers to customize their approach based on the specific environment they are targeting, making it particularly resilient against traditional cybersecurity measures. The architecture is characterized by a multi-layered approach that includes a command and control (C2) infrastructure, encryption methods, and a user-friendly interface for transactions.

The command and control infrastructure of BitPaymer is pivotal in its operational effectiveness. The ransomware relies on a distributed network of C2 servers, which are often hosted on compromised servers or cloud services. This decentralization not only enhances redundancy but also complicates efforts to dismantle the network. The C2 servers are responsible for delivering critical updates to the ransomware, managing the encryption keys, and facilitating communication between the malware and the attackers. This allows for real-time monitoring of infected systems and the ability to adjust tactics as needed, such as increasing ransom demands or altering encryption methods based on the victim's response.

Encryption is another crucial aspect of BitPaymer's technical architecture. The ransomware employs a strong encryption algorithm, typically utilizing the AES (Advanced Encryption Standard) in conjunction with RSA (Rivest–Shamir–Adleman) for key exchange. This dual-layer encryption ensures that files are not only locked but that the decryption keys remain securely stored on the attackers' servers. The use of robust encryption methods makes it exceedingly difficult for victims to recover their files without paying the ransom, as brute-force decryption attempts are rendered impractical due to the time and computational power required.

The user interface of BitPaymer is designed to facilitate communication with victims in a streamlined manner. The ransomware typically generates a ransom note that is displayed upon successful encryption of the victim's files. This note provides clear instructions on how to proceed with the payment, often utilizing cryptocurrencies like Bitcoin to ensure anonymity for the attackers. The interface may also include a countdown timer, adding psychological pressure on the victim to comply quickly. By making the payment process straightforward, BitPaymer increases the likelihood that victims will opt to pay the ransom rather than attempt recovery through more conventional means.

Finally, the evolution of BitPaymer's architecture reflects a broader trend in ransomware development, where attackers continually refine their methods to stay ahead of cybersecurity defenses. As the landscape of cybersecurity evolves, so too do the tactics employed by ransomware developers. The technical architecture of BitPaymer illustrates how these malicious actors leverage advanced technologies and innovative strategies to maximize their impact. Understanding this architecture is essential for cybersecurity professionals who must develop effective defenses and response strategies to protect against such complex threats.

Attack Vectors and Delivery Methods

Understanding attack vectors and delivery methods is crucial for cybersecurity professionals seeking to mitigate risks associated with ransomware, particularly in the context of Dridex and BitPaymer. These two ransomware strains have evolved from sophisticated malware ecosystems, utilizing a variety of tactics to infiltrate and compromise target environments. A comprehensive analysis of these attack vectors reveals the multifaceted approaches employed by Evil Corp, the notorious group behind these threats.

Phishing remains one of the primary attack vectors for Dridex and BitPaymer. Cybercriminals often leverage social engineering techniques to craft convincing emails that entice users to click on malicious links or download infected attachments. These phishing campaigns are typically designed to mimic legitimate communications from trusted entities, thereby increasing the likelihood of user interaction. Once the malware is executed, it can establish a foothold within the network, enabling further exploitation and lateral movement.

Another significant delivery method employed by Evil Corp is the use of exploit kits. These kits are designed to take advantage of vulnerabilities in software applications and operating systems. By embedding malicious code within compromised websites, attackers can distribute their payload to unsuspecting visitors. Exploit kits automate the process of identifying system vulnerabilities, making them a highly effective tool for delivering ransomware. As such, maintaining up-to-date software and employing robust patch management practices are essential defensive measures.

Remote Desktop Protocol (RDP) exploitation has also emerged as a favored technique for ransomware delivery. Cybercriminals often scan for exposed RDP ports and utilize credential stuffing or brute-force attacks to gain unauthorized access to systems. Once inside, they can deploy ransomware directly onto the network, often escalating privileges to maximize their impact. This method underscores the importance of implementing strong authentication measures and network segmentation to safeguard critical assets.

Finally, the rise of Ransomware as a Service (RaaS) has transformed the ransomware landscape, allowing even less technically skilled criminals to launch attacks. Evil Corp has capitalized on this model, providing access to their ransomware strains for a fee. This commercialization of ransomware creates a broader threat surface, as it enables a diverse array of attackers to utilize sophisticated tools and tactics. Cybersecurity professionals must remain vigilant to detect and respond to these evolving threats, employing a layered security approach that includes user education, technical controls, and incident response planning to mitigate potential impacts.

Impact of BitPaymer on Organizations

BitPaymer has significantly impacted organizations across various sectors, primarily through its sophisticated execution of ransomware attacks. Its modus operandi involves infiltrating corporate networks, often through phishing or exploiting vulnerabilities, and subsequently encrypting critical files. Once the data is held hostage, victims receive a ransom demand, typically in cryptocurrency, which complicates tracing and recovery efforts. The alarming success of BitPaymer has not only resulted in substantial financial losses for affected organizations but has also prompted a reevaluation of cybersecurity strategies and incident response protocols.

The financial ramifications of BitPaymer attacks extend beyond immediate ransom payments. Organizations often face additional costs related to recovery efforts, such as data restoration, system repairs, and potential regulatory fines due to data breaches. Furthermore, businesses may suffer reputational damage that can lead to a loss of customer trust and, consequently, a decline in revenue. The fear of future attacks also leads many organizations to invest heavily in cybersecurity infrastructure, reflecting a growing recognition of the need to fortify defenses against such sophisticated threats.

BitPaymer exemplifies the evolution of ransomware into a business model that thrives on exploiting vulnerabilities within organizational frameworks. The attack vector used by BitPaymer highlights the importance of robust security measures, including employee training on phishing awareness and the implementation of multi-factor authentication. Organizations are increasingly recognizing that the human element is often the weakest link in cybersecurity. As a result, comprehensive training programs are being developed to equip employees with the skills necessary to identify and mitigate potential threats before they can be exploited.

The rise of BitPaymer has also underscored the necessity for effective incident response strategies. Organizations that have fallen victim to BitPaymer often report that their initial response was hampered by a lack of preparedness and clear protocols. Lessons learned from these incidents emphasize the importance of having a well-defined incident response plan that includes not just technical recovery but also communication strategies for stakeholders. This proactive approach can significantly mitigate damage and facilitate quicker recovery, ultimately reducing the overall impact of a ransomware attack.

In conclusion, the impact of BitPaymer on organizations has been profound, serving as a wake-up call for cybersecurity professionals. The lessons learned from attacks attributed to this ransomware emphasize the importance of a multi-faceted approach to cybersecurity that includes technological defenses, employee training, and robust incident response strategies. As the landscape of ransomware continues to evolve, organizations must remain vigilant and adaptable, ensuring they are equipped to face the challenges posed by sophisticated threats like BitPaymer.

Chapter 7: Ransomware as a Service

Business Models of Evil Corp

The business models employed by Evil Corp represent a sophisticated and lucrative approach to cybercrime, particularly in the realms of Dridex and BitPaymer ransomware. Central to their operations is a tiered structure that allows for the maximization of profits while minimizing risk. This model is designed to leverage both technology and human resources, enabling the organization to execute attacks with precision and efficiency. Each facet of their business strategy is carefully crafted to ensure sustainability and growth in a rapidly evolving cyber threat landscape.

One of the primary components of Evil Corp's business model is the concept of Ransomware as a Service (RaaS). This model democratizes access to sophisticated ransomware tools, allowing even less technically skilled criminals to launch attacks. By providing a platform that includes ready-to-deploy ransomware, tutorials, and customer support, Evil Corp can tap into a broader market of cybercriminals. This not only increases the volume of attacks but also generates a continuous stream of revenue through licensing fees and profit-sharing arrangements with affiliates who deploy their ransomware.

Another significant aspect of Evil Corp's operations is their use of targeted phishing campaigns to distribute malware like Dridex. These campaigns are meticulously planned and executed, often utilizing social engineering tactics to lure victims into unwittingly downloading malicious software. By focusing on specific industries or organizations, Evil Corp can enhance the effectiveness of their attacks, increasing the likelihood of successful infiltration and subsequent ransom demands. This strategic targeting is coupled with data exfiltration tactics that amplify their leverage over victims, as stolen data can be used for both extortion and resale on dark web marketplaces.

The evolutionary aspect of Evil Corp's business model is evident in their adaptability to law enforcement measures and cybersecurity advancements. As organizations enhance their defenses, Evil Corp has pivoted to employ more sophisticated evasion techniques, such as the use of encrypted communication channels and decentralized infrastructure. This adaptability not only prolongs the life cycle of their ransomware but also ensures that their operations can continue to thrive despite increasing pressure from cybersecurity professionals and law enforcement agencies.

Ultimately, the business models of Evil Corp highlight the need for a comprehensive and proactive approach to incident response and cybersecurity strategies. Understanding the intricacies of how these cybercriminal organizations operate can provide crucial insights for cybersecurity professionals tasked with defending against such threats. By analyzing the methods and motivations of Evil Corp, professionals can better prepare their organizations to recognize, respond to, and recover from ransomware incidents, ultimately mitigating the risks associated with such attacks.

Marketplaces and Distribution Channels

In the realm of cybercrime, understanding the marketplaces and distribution channels utilized by organizations like Evil Corp is crucial for cybersecurity professionals. These entities have developed sophisticated methods for distributing ransomware, particularly Dridex and BitPaymer, through a network of underground platforms. These marketplaces serve as hubs for cybercriminals to trade tools, stolen data, and ransomware-as-a-service (RaaS) offerings. Each platform operates under a veil of anonymity, facilitating transactions that are often encrypted and obfuscated to evade law enforcement detection.

The distribution of ransomware typically begins with the compromise of legitimate systems, often through phishing campaigns or exploiting software vulnerabilities. Once access is gained, the ransomware is deployed, and the infection spreads through internal networks. Evil Corp has effectively utilized these methods to maximize their reach, often employing affiliate programs where other cybercriminals can purchase and deploy ransomware in exchange for a cut of the ransom payments. This decentralized approach allows Evil Corp to scale their operations while minimizing risk, as they rely on a network of affiliates to carry out attacks.

Marketplaces like the dark web provide a variety of services that support these operations, including forums for sharing tactics, techniques, and procedures (TTPs). Cybersecurity professionals must be aware of these platforms, as they are breeding grounds for innovation in ransomware deployment. The anonymity provided by cryptocurrencies, such as Bitcoin, further complicates the tracking of financial transactions associated with ransomware payments. Understanding the landscape of these marketplaces enables security teams to anticipate potential threats and develop countermeasures against evolving ransomware tactics.

Furthermore, the distribution channels extend beyond mere ransomware deployment. They encompass a broader ecosystem, including the sale of stolen credentials, access to compromised networks, and the exchange of malware development resources. Evil Corp and similar organizations thrive in this environment by maintaining relationships with various vendors and affiliates, creating a robust supply chain of cybercrime. This interconnectedness can make incident response challenging, as attacks may originate from multiple sources, each with its own set of motivations and methodologies.

To combat the growing threat posed by ransomware distributed through such sophisticated channels, cybersecurity professionals must adopt a proactive stance. This includes constant monitoring of emerging marketplaces, understanding the flow of ransomware-as-a-service, and developing comprehensive incident response plans that account for the complexities of these distribution channels. By keeping abreast of the tactics employed by organizations like Evil Corp, cybersecurity teams can better protect their organizations against the dangers posed by Dridex, BitPaymer, and the evolving landscape of ransomware.

Partnerships and Affiliates

Partnerships and affiliates play a crucial role in the operational dynamics of Evil Corp, particularly in the context of their ransomware ventures like Dridex and BitPaymer. These relationships extend the reach of their malicious activities, enhance their capabilities, and facilitate the dissemination of their ransomware products. By collaborating with various affiliates, Evil Corp can leverage a diverse range of skills, resources, and networks, making their operations more resilient and adaptable to law enforcement efforts. Understanding these partnerships is essential for cybersecurity professionals aiming to dismantle these organizations and mitigate their impact on the digital landscape.

Evil Corp has established a robust affiliate program that incentivizes third parties to promote and distribute their ransomware. This model typically operates on a revenue-sharing basis, where affiliates receive a percentage of the ransom payments collected from victims. Such arrangements not only expand the operational footprint of Evil Corp but also create an ecosystem in which affiliates are motivated to innovate and optimize their attack strategies. This decentralized approach allows Evil Corp to maintain a degree of plausible deniability while effectively outsourcing critical aspects of their ransomware campaigns to independent operators.

The evolution of ransomware has seen an increase in partnerships with various cybercriminal entities, including those specializing in malware development, infrastructure support, and money laundering. By collaborating with experts in these areas, Evil Corp enhances the sophistication of its attacks and improves its operational efficiency. For instance, partnerships with malware developers may lead to the creation of more effective encryption algorithms, while relationships with money laundering networks ensure that ransom payments are swiftly converted into untraceable assets. Such collaborations underscore the need for cybersecurity professionals to adopt a comprehensive understanding of the interconnected nature of cybercrime.

The implications of these partnerships extend beyond immediate operational concerns; they also pose significant challenges for incident response teams. Cybersecurity professionals must recognize that addressing the threat posed by Evil Corp and its affiliates requires a multi-faceted approach. This includes not only technical measures to mitigate ransomware attacks but also strategic initiatives aimed at disrupting the networks and partnerships that enable these criminals. By dismantling the affiliate programs and severing the connections between Evil Corp and its partners, incident responders can significantly weaken the organization's operational capabilities.

In conclusion, the partnerships and affiliates of Evil Corp represent a complex web of relationships that drive the evolution and implementation of ransomware like Dridex and BitPaymer. Cybersecurity professionals must remain vigilant and informed about these dynamics to effectively combat the threats posed by such organizations. By understanding the role of partnerships in ransomware operations, professionals can develop targeted strategies that address both the technical and operational aspects of this pervasive threat, ultimately enhancing their ability to protect organizations from the devastating impacts of ransomware.

Chapter 8: Incident Response Strategies

Preparation and Prevention

Preparation and prevention are critical components in the cybersecurity landscape, particularly when addressing the threats posed by sophisticated ransomware groups such as Evil Corp. Cybersecurity professionals must understand the nuances of these threats to effectively mitigate risks and bolster defenses. A proactive approach includes not only the development of robust security measures but also the cultivation of an organizational culture centered on cybersecurity awareness. This involves training employees to recognize phishing attempts, which are often the initial vectors for ransomware like Dridex and BitPaymer.

To combat the evolving tactics employed by Evil Corp, organizations should implement a multi-layered security strategy. This includes deploying advanced endpoint protection, utilizing network segmentation, and enforcing strict access controls. Regularly updating and patching software can significantly reduce vulnerabilities that attackers exploit. Furthermore, organizations must prioritize the integration of threat intelligence to stay informed about the latest ransomware developments and trends. By understanding the modus operandi of Dridex and BitPaymer, cybersecurity professionals can develop targeted defenses that are adaptive to changing threat landscapes.

Regular risk assessments and penetration testing play a pivotal role in preparation efforts. By simulating potential attack scenarios, organizations can identify weaknesses in their security posture and address them before actual breaches occur. These assessments should be comprehensive, examining not only technical controls but also operational processes and employee behavior. Developing incident response plans that incorporate lessons learned from previous attacks can enhance an organization's resilience against ransomware incidents. It is essential that these plans are regularly reviewed and updated to reflect the current threat environment.

In addition to technical and procedural defenses, fostering a culture of cybersecurity is vital for prevention. Employees are often the first line of defense; thus, their awareness and training significantly impact an organization's vulnerability to ransomware attacks. Implementing regular training sessions and phishing simulations can empower employees to recognize and report suspicious activity. Moreover, organizations should encourage a transparent reporting culture where employees feel safe to report potential security issues without fear of repercussion. This proactive engagement can significantly contribute to a more robust security posture.

Finally, collaboration with external partners and cybersecurity communities can amplify preparation and prevention efforts. Sharing threat intelligence and best practices with peers in the industry can provide invaluable insights into emerging threats and effective countermeasures. Participating in information-sharing platforms allows organizations to collectively enhance their defenses against the tactics employed by Evil Corp and similar entities. By fostering a collaborative environment, cybersecurity professionals can create a more resilient framework not just for their organizations but for the broader ecosystem facing the persistent threat of ransomware.

Detection and Analysis

Detection and analysis are critical components in the battle against ransomware, particularly with threats like Dridex and BitPaymer, which have become synonymous with advanced cybercriminal tactics. Cybersecurity professionals must adopt a multifaceted approach that combines traditional detection methods with modern analytical techniques to effectively identify and mitigate the risks posed by these sophisticated threats. This subchapter delves into the strategies employed to detect these ransomware variants and the analytical frameworks utilized to understand their operational methodologies.

To effectively detect Dridex and BitPaymer, organizations must implement comprehensive threat intelligence solutions that continuously monitor network traffic and endpoints for indicators of compromise. The use of behavioral analysis plays a significant role in this process, as it allows security teams to identify anomalies that may signal the presence of ransomware. Machine learning models can be particularly useful in recognizing patterns consistent with the activities of Evil Corp, such as specific file modifications, unusual network connections, and the use of known command-and-control servers. By integrating these technologies into their security infrastructure, professionals can enhance their ability to detect ransomware before it executes a full-scale attack.

In addition to detection techniques, thorough analysis of ransomware incidents is crucial for understanding the evolution of these threats. For instance, analyzing the attack vectors used by Dridex and BitPaymer reveals a reliance on social engineering tactics, such as phishing emails and malicious attachments. By dissecting these vectors, cybersecurity professionals can better educate their workforce about the risks associated with human error and implement more effective training programs. Moreover, analyzing the ransomware's code and encryption methods helps security teams develop decryption tools and recovery strategies, which are vital for incident response efforts.

The business models employed by Evil Corp, particularly the Ransomware as a Service (RaaS) model, also warrant detailed examination during the analysis phase. Understanding how these cybercriminal organizations operate and monetize their attacks can provide insights into their motivations and future tactics. By recognizing the subscription-based nature of RaaS, cybersecurity professionals can anticipate potential threats and prepare defenses accordingly. This situational awareness is essential for mitigating the risks associated with ransomware, as it enables organizations to stay one step ahead of the evolving landscape.

Finally, lessons learned from past incidents involving Dridex and BitPaymer underscore the importance of continuous improvement in detection and analysis strategies. Post-incident reviews and threat hunting exercises can help identify gaps in existing security measures and inform future practices. Engaging in collaborative efforts with law enforcement and industry peers can also facilitate the sharing of intelligence, leading to a more robust understanding of the methods used by Evil Corp and similar groups. By fostering a culture of proactive detection and thorough analysis, cybersecurity professionals can significantly enhance their defenses against ransomware threats.

Containment and Eradication

Containment and eradication are critical phases in the incident response process, particularly when dealing with sophisticated ransomware attacks like those orchestrated by Evil Corp through the Dridex and BitPaymer strains. For cybersecurity professionals, understanding the nuances of these phases can significantly mitigate damage and enhance recovery efforts. Containment involves restricting the spread of the ransomware, while eradication focuses on completely removing the threat from the environment. These steps require a well-defined strategy, informed by an understanding of the attack vectors utilized by Evil Corp.

An essential aspect of containment is the identification of affected systems and the swift isolation of these assets from the network. This may involve shutting down or quarantining machines exhibiting signs of compromise, such as unusual file encryption activities or unauthorized access attempts. In the context of Dridex and BitPaymer, which are known for their lateral movement capabilities, rapid detection and isolation are vital to prevent the ransomware from propagating to other devices. Cybersecurity professionals must leverage advanced monitoring tools and threat intelligence to identify indicators of compromise (IoCs) associated with these ransomware variants.

Once containment is achieved, the focus shifts to eradication, which necessitates a thorough analysis of the malware's behavior and its entry points. In the case of Dridex and BitPaymer, which often exploit vulnerabilities in software or employ phishing tactics for initial access, a comprehensive review of security protocols is essential. This includes patching software vulnerabilities, enhancing email filtering mechanisms, and educating users about social engineering threats. The goal is not only to eliminate the current threat but also to fortify the organization against future attacks, making it imperative for cybersecurity teams to document their findings and adjust their security posture accordingly.

Moreover, the eradication phase should involve a meticulous cleanup process to ensure that no remnants of the ransomware remain in the environment. This may include the deployment of endpoint detection and response (EDR) solutions to scan and remediate infected systems. Additionally, cybersecurity professionals must consider the potential for backdoors or secondary payloads that could be left behind by the attackers. By performing a thorough forensic analysis, organizations can recover from incidents more effectively and develop actionable insights to prevent similar breaches in the future.

Finally, following the containment and eradication processes, a comprehensive review and post-incident analysis are crucial. This allows cybersecurity professionals to evaluate the effectiveness of their response strategies and identify areas for improvement. Lessons learned from incidents involving Dridex and BitPaymer can inform future training and preparedness efforts, ultimately leading to a more resilient cybersecurity framework. Emphasizing the importance of continuous improvement in incident response not only ensures better preparedness for future ransomware threats but also reinforces the overarching goal of safeguarding organizational assets against evolving cyber threats.

Chapter 9: Lessons Learned from Dridex and BitPaymer Attacks

Case Studies of Major Incidents

The case studies of major incidents associated with Evil Corp and its notorious ransomware, Dridex and BitPaymer, provide critical insights into the operational methodologies and impact of these cybercriminal enterprises. One of the most significant incidents occurred in 2015, when Dridex first emerged as a banking Trojan. Its primary function was to steal personal information and financial data from victims. By leveraging sophisticated phishing techniques, attackers successfully compromised numerous corporate accounts, leading to substantial financial losses. The incident highlighted the effectiveness of social engineering tactics in infiltrating organizations, demonstrating the need for enhanced email security protocols and employee training to recognize phishing attempts.

In 2019, the BitPaymer ransomware gained notoriety for its aggressive tactics and targeted approach, primarily aimed at healthcare institutions and municipalities. One notable case involved a major healthcare provider that was paralyzed by the ransomware, resulting in the shutdown of critical systems and a significant disruption of services. The attackers demanded a large ransom, and the incident underscored the vulnerability of essential services to ransomware attacks. This case prompted a reevaluation of incident response strategies, emphasizing the importance of maintaining robust backups and implementing comprehensive disaster recovery plans to mitigate potential damages from such incidents.

The evolution of ransomware from simple encryption attacks to sophisticated, multi-faceted operations can be traced through incidents involving both Dridex and BitPaymer. For example, the transition from purely financial theft to ransomware delivery systems marked a significant shift in the cybercrime landscape. By analyzing these incidents, cybersecurity professionals can recognize patterns in attacker behavior and evolving tactics. This knowledge is crucial for developing proactive defenses and improving threat intelligence capabilities, allowing organizations to stay ahead of potential attacks.

Additionally, the business model of ransomware as a service (RaaS) has emerged as a key component of Evil Corp's operations. The accessibility of ransomware tools for less technically skilled criminals has led to an increase in the volume and variety of attacks. Case studies of incidents involving RaaS demonstrate the effectiveness of affiliate programs, where experienced developers provide tools and support to less skilled attackers. This model not only amplifies the threat landscape but also complicates attribution efforts, making it more challenging for cybersecurity professionals to identify and respond to threats.

Finally, the lessons learned from the Dridex and BitPaymer attacks emphasize the need for a coordinated approach to incident response and recovery. Organizations must prioritize collaboration between IT, legal, and public relations teams to effectively manage the fallout from ransomware incidents. The analysis of past incidents reveals the critical role of communication in maintaining stakeholder trust and ensuring a swift recovery. By studying these case studies, cybersecurity professionals can refine their incident response strategies, ensuring they are better equipped to handle the evolving threat posed by ransomware and cybercriminal organizations like Evil Corp.

Best Practices for Cybersecurity Professionals

Best practices for cybersecurity professionals in the context of evolving threats like Dridex and BitPaymer ransomware are essential for building robust defenses and ensuring organizational resilience. First and foremost, continuous education and training are paramount. Cybersecurity is a rapidly changing field, and professionals must stay informed about the latest attack vectors, malware variants, and emerging trends. Regularly participating in workshops, webinars, and certification programs can enhance skill sets and provide fresh insights into the tactics employed by threat actors. Moreover, fostering a culture of awareness within organizations ensures that all employees are vigilant and equipped to recognize potential threats.

Another critical best practice involves implementing a layered security approach, often referred to as defense in depth. This strategy utilizes multiple security measures at various levels of an organization's infrastructure to protect against breaches. By combining firewalls, intrusion detection systems, endpoint protection, and email filtering, cybersecurity professionals can create a more formidable barrier against ransomware attacks. Additionally, employing network segmentation can limit the spread of malware if a breach does occur, thereby minimizing damage and facilitating quicker recovery.

Regular data backups are also a cornerstone of effective cybersecurity practices. Professionals must ensure that data is backed up frequently and stored securely, ideally in an offline or cloud-based environment. This practice not only helps recover data in case of a ransomware attack but also serves as a proactive measure against data loss due to other incidents such as hardware failures or natural disasters. Testing the backup and recovery process is equally important to ensure that it functions correctly when needed most, thus reducing downtime and impact on business operations.

Incident response planning is another crucial area where cybersecurity professionals must excel. Developing and regularly updating an incident response plan is vital for effectively managing ransomware incidents. This plan should outline specific procedures for detection, containment, eradication, and recovery from an attack. Conducting tabletop exercises and simulations can prepare teams for real-world scenarios, enhancing their ability to respond quickly and efficiently when an incident occurs. Learning from past incidents, such as those involving Dridex and BitPaymer, can provide valuable insights into refining these plans and addressing any gaps in response capabilities.

Finally, collaboration and information sharing among cybersecurity professionals and organizations are essential for combating ransomware threats. Engaging with industry groups, threat intelligence sharing platforms, and law enforcement can help professionals stay informed about new threats and tactics. By sharing knowledge about vulnerabilities, attack patterns, and effective countermeasures, the cybersecurity community can strengthen its collective defenses against sophisticated adversaries like those behind Dridex and BitPaymer. Building a network of trusted contacts for support during incidents can further enhance response capabilities and foster a united front against the evolving landscape of ransomware attacks.

Future Trends in Ransomware and Cybersecurity

The landscape of ransomware continues to evolve, presenting new challenges and opportunities for cybersecurity professionals. As cybercriminals become more sophisticated, the future of ransomware will likely see an increased reliance on automation and artificial intelligence. This shift could enable attackers to execute more targeted and efficient attacks, reducing the time it takes to compromise a network and deploy ransomware. Cybersecurity teams must adapt by incorporating advanced threat detection and response capabilities that leverage machine learning and behavioral analysis to identify and mitigate these threats proactively.

One notable trend is the emergence of Ransomware as a Service (RaaS), which lowers the barrier to entry for cybercriminals. This model allows individuals with varying technical skills to launch ransomware attacks by utilizing pre-built kits available on dark web marketplaces. As RaaS continues to gain traction, cybersecurity professionals will need to develop strategies to address not just the attacks themselves but also the underlying ecosystem that supports these criminal enterprises. This includes monitoring dark web activities and collaborating with law enforcement to disrupt RaaS operations.

The increasing use of cryptocurrency for ransom payments poses another significant challenge. The anonymity features of cryptocurrencies make it difficult for law enforcement to trace payments back to the perpetrators. As ransomware attacks become more prevalent, there may be a push for regulatory changes regarding cryptocurrency exchanges to enhance traceability and accountability. Cybersecurity professionals should be prepared to engage in discussions about these regulatory frameworks and consider how they can influence policy to deter ransomware payments and support victims.

Furthermore, as organizations continue to embrace cloud technologies, the attack surface for ransomware is expanding.

Attackers are likely to target cloud infrastructure and services, exploiting misconfigurations and vulnerabilities to deploy ransomware. This trend highlights the need for robust cloud security measures and comprehensive incident response plans. Cybersecurity teams must prioritize cloud security best practices, including regular audits, access controls, and continuous monitoring to protect against potential ransomware threats.

Finally, the human element remains a critical factor in the fight against ransomware. Social engineering tactics are expected to become more sophisticated, making it imperative for organizations to invest in employee training and awareness programs. Cybersecurity professionals should focus on cultivating a security-aware culture within their organizations, where employees are equipped to recognize phishing attempts and other tactics used by ransomware operators. By addressing both technological and human vulnerabilities, organizations can build a more resilient defense against the evolving threat of ransomware.

Chapter 10: Conclusion

Reflection on Evil Corp's Impact

Evil Corp, a notorious group implicated in the creation of Dridex and BitPaymer ransomware, has significantly altered the landscape of cybersecurity. Their operations exemplify the evolution of ransomware from simple malware to sophisticated, organized criminal enterprises. By leveraging advanced technology and adopting business models reminiscent of legitimate corporations, Evil Corp has transformed the way ransomware is deployed, making it a lucrative venture for cybercriminals. Their impact extends beyond immediate financial gains, as they have catalyzed a broader discussion on the necessity for robust cybersecurity measures and the importance of understanding the motivations behind such attacks.

The architecture of Dridex and BitPaymer provides critical insights into the operational tactics employed by Evil Corp. Dridex, initially designed as a banking Trojan, evolved to exploit vulnerabilities in systems worldwide, demonstrating a remarkable adaptability. Similarly, BitPaymer showcased the group's ability to capitalize on existing infrastructures, employing a targeted approach to infiltrate organizations and hold their data hostage. This evolution signifies a shift towards more aggressive tactics, where ransomware is not only a tool for financial gain but also a means of exerting psychological pressure on victims. Cybersecurity professionals must analyze these patterns to better anticipate and mitigate future threats.

The emergence of ransomware as a service (RaaS) has further complicated the response landscape. Evil Corp has effectively democratized access to sophisticated ransomware tools, allowing less technically skilled criminals to participate in cyber extortion. This model not only increases the volume of attacks but also diversifies the types of organizations targeted, ranging from small businesses to large enterprises. Understanding this business model is crucial for cybersecurity professionals, as it underscores the importance of proactive measures and collaboration across industries to combat the proliferation of ransomware.

Incident response strategies have evolved in response to the tactics employed by Evil Corp. The lessons learned from Dridex and BitPaymer attacks highlight the necessity for comprehensive incident response plans that incorporate threat intelligence and real-time monitoring. Organizations must invest in training for cybersecurity teams, emphasizing the importance of rapid detection and response capabilities. Additionally, collaboration with law enforcement and sharing of threat intelligence can enhance the collective defense against such sophisticated attacks, fostering a more resilient cybersecurity community.

The impact of Evil Corp transcends individual attacks, prompting a reevaluation of cybersecurity priorities across various sectors. Their operations have illustrated the need for an adaptive defense strategy that anticipates the evolving nature of cyber threats. As ransomware continues to thrive, cybersecurity professionals must remain vigilant, embracing innovation and collaboration to safeguard against the sophisticated tactics employed by groups like Evil Corp. Acknowledging their influence on the ransomware landscape is essential for developing effective defenses and ensuring the long-term security of organizational assets.

The Future of Ransomware

The landscape of ransomware is continuously evolving, driven by technological advancements and the increasing sophistication of cybercriminals. As we look to the future, it is essential for cybersecurity professionals to understand the potential trajectories of ransomware threats. The emergence of Ransomware as a Service (RaaS) has democratized access to these malicious tools, enabling even less experienced criminals to launch sophisticated attacks. This shift not only broadens the attack surface but also complicates the defensive strategies that organizations must employ.

Evil Corp, the notorious group behind Dridex and BitPaymer, exemplifies how organized cybercrime has adapted to exploit vulnerabilities in both technology and human behavior. Their business model integrates elements of traditional enterprise practices, such as customer support and continuous software updates, which enhances the effectiveness of their ransomware operations. As future iterations of ransomware emerge, it is likely that similar groups will adopt hybrid approaches, blending technical advancements with social engineering tactics to increase their success rates.

In addition to the technical advancements in ransomware, the regulatory environment is also shifting. Governments worldwide are responding to the rise in ransomware attacks by implementing stricter regulations and penalties for organizations that fail to protect their data. This changing landscape creates pressure on organizations to adopt more robust cybersecurity measures. Cybersecurity professionals must stay ahead of these regulations and ensure compliance while balancing the need for effective incident response strategies.

Education and awareness will play a crucial role in mitigating future ransomware threats. Cybersecurity professionals must prioritize training programs that not only cover technical defenses but also address the human factors that contribute to successful attacks. As ransomware tactics evolve, so too must the strategies employed to counter them. This includes fostering a culture of cybersecurity within organizations where employees are empowered to recognize and report suspicious activities.

Finally, the future of ransomware will likely see increased collaboration between cybercriminals and other illicit actors, such as data brokers and exploit developers. This interconnectedness can lead to more sophisticated and targeted attacks, making it imperative for cybersecurity professionals to engage in threat intelligence sharing and collaboration. By understanding the tactics, techniques, and procedures of groups like Evil Corp, the cybersecurity community can better prepare for the challenges that lie ahead, ultimately reducing the impact of ransomware on organizations and individuals alike.

Final Thoughts for Cybersecurity Professionals

As cybersecurity professionals, it is imperative to recognize the profound impact that entities like Evil Corp have on the digital landscape. The evolution of ransomware, particularly with the Dridex and BitPaymer strains, underscores the sophistication and adaptability of cybercriminals. Understanding their operational models—especially the Ransomware as a Service (RaaS) structure—provides valuable insights into how these threats are disseminated and magnified. The ease with which these services are offered in underground markets heightens the urgency for professionals to stay informed and vigilant.

The key players behind Dridex and BitPaymer exemplify the need for ongoing education and collaboration within the cybersecurity community. Their ability to innovate and refine tactics, techniques, and procedures (TTPs) presents a constant challenge for defenders. By analyzing their approaches, cybersecurity experts can develop more effective strategies for incident response, threat hunting, and risk mitigation. It is essential to maintain a proactive stance in learning from previous incidents and adapting defenses accordingly.

Ransomware as a Service has transformed the ransomware landscape, making it accessible to a wider range of attackers with varying skill levels. This democratization of cybercrime means that the threat is more pervasive than ever. Cybersecurity professionals must not only understand the technical aspects of these attacks but also the underlying business models that drive them. Awareness of these dynamics can facilitate better risk assessments and inform the development of tailored security measures to protect organizations from such threats.

Incident response is an area where lessons learned from the attacks associated with Evil Corp can significantly enhance preparedness. Establishing robust incident response plans and conducting regular simulations can help organizations respond more effectively when faced with ransomware incidents. Cybersecurity teams should prioritize building a culture of preparedness, ensuring that all employees understand their roles in the event of an attack. The insights gained from analyzing past incidents can guide the refinement of these plans, making them more resilient to evolving threats.

In conclusion, the ongoing battle against ransomware requires a concerted effort from cybersecurity professionals to adapt and evolve. The insights gathered from studying Evil Corp and its operations provide a crucial foundation for developing effective defenses against future attacks. By fostering a collaborative environment, sharing knowledge, and leveraging lessons learned, the cybersecurity community can build a more formidable front against the ever-evolving threat landscape of ransomware. The path forward demands vigilance, innovation, and a commitment to continuous improvement in the face of adversity.